Warning-Disclaimer

The purpose of this book is to educate and entertain. The author or publisher does not guarantee that anyone following the techniques, suggestions, tips, ideas, or strategies will become successful. The author and publisher shall have neither liability or responsibility to anyone with respect to any loss or damage caused, or alleged to be caused, directly or indirectly by the information contained in this book.

CONTENTS

3

INTRODUCTION

Everybody's talking about the Instant Pot. Literally everyone! Look on Pinterest, read reviews on Amazon: The Instant Pot. Is. Everywhere.

Before we tried it, I heard that a soup normally ready in 6-8 hours in the slow cooker is ready in 15-30 minutes in the Instant Pot! Crazy, right?

The Instant Pot is fully programmable, so you can simply set the timer and then do other jobs without having to keep an eye on it. Because it's a pressure cooker, it really does work much, much faster than a traditional crockpot. Plus, you can set the Instant Pot timer so it will start and end when you want dinner ready. Pretty convenient.

14 Instant Pot Tips and Tricks

1. Read up on all the functions before you start
We all love jumping in and getting started, especially when we buy a new cooking "toy," but definitely (definitely!) read up on the instructions and details before you embark on your Instant Pot cooking. It's a little different and requires getting used to. You'll experience more success if you do your homework beforehand.

2. Use plenty of liquid
Pressure cooking is all about steam, so your food needs plenty of moisture to heat up. The Instant Pot works well for soups and sauces. While not much moisture will be lost during cooking, it's not a dry heat. You won't get a crust or crispiness from the Instant Pot.

3. Food cooks by surface area rather than volume
Big foods like a roast or a large potato will cook slower than foods cut into smaller pieces. The steam and pressure must reach the inside of each piece of food, so if you want to speed up your cooking time, cut food into smaller pieces.

4. Plan before you cook
Be sure to read through recipes before getting started. Some recipes will call for extra supplies—i.e. a spring-form pan, different sealant rings (for use with different foods) or a steamer insert, which you'll need to purchase separately. Set the Pot to "sealing" rather than "venting," if you're cooking food.

5. Don't overfill

Keep in mind, heat and liquid can cause some foods to swell and expand (like beans). Only fill your Instant Pot up to the fill line and leave plenty of room to accommodate for expanding rice, beans, quinoa, and other legumes and grains. For slow cooker recipes, you'll want to keep the liquid to 1-2 cups (no less than 1).

6. Use separate sealing rings
One of the only areas of the Instant Pot to take on odor are the inner seal rings. You can use different sealing rings for savory foods (like curry, garlic or spiced foods) and for sweet or mild foods (like fruits, desserts and oatmeal). This will prevent the rings from taking on or transferring food scents.

7. Prepare ingredients in large quantities
The Instant Pot really shines if you need to prepare a lot of one thing—like a few dozen boiled eggs or chicken breasts. Cook meat like chicken ahead by adding broth or water and a few herbs. You can then shred the meat to use in tacos, casseroles or as you would use rotisserie chicken or pulled pork.

8. Use the steaming insert for quicker cooking foods
You can add quicker cooking foods later (you just need to depressurize your Instant Pot before opening it). Use the steamer insert or a heat-safe ceramic, metal or glass bowl. You can also add food wrapped in foil. If you open the Instant Pot to add an ingredient, it will reheat much faster. You can also use the steaming insert for eggs.

9. Use caution with dairy and cheese (unless you're making yogurt)
The Instant Pot works great for making yogurt (see our recipe link below) but it doesn't always do as well with creamy sauces and cheese. While pasta cooks fast, making it great for pasta recipes, milk can scald and cheese gets gloppy and watery. The rapid heat can also cause milk to curdle in some cases. When making a creamy recipe, add dairy such as milk, cream and soft cheese after the pressure cooking process (stir in at the end, using the sauté function) for better results.

10. Thicken after cooking
Because there isn't much liquid lost during the cooking process, you may need to add a slurry (cornstarch whisked with water) or another thickener to sauces after the meal is finished cooking. Don't add thickener like cornstarch or flour into the Instant Pot, as it's too difficult to control the thickening process and can interfere with the steam. Another option is to remove a portion of the liquid after cooking and set the Instant Pot to sauté. I've found this works well with "meat and sauce" based dishes.

11. Delay cooking with the timer

Delay your cooking start time using the timing feature to get dishes ready when YOU want them. You can use the delay timing feature to start the Instant Pot at any time or to keep food warm after cooking. Because the Instant Pot is so fast, you don't have to wait for meals to defrost or plan so far in advance. Most meals (even roasts) are ready in less than an hour. Some are ready in 10 minutes or less!

12. Keep in mind the lid locks

One slightly tricky feature to keep in mind is the Instant Pot seals as soon as pressure begins. So, if you forget an ingredient or need to add ingredients in stages, give it time to depressurize and let off the steam. This can be a problem if you suddenly realize you forgot to add onions to the soup or spices to your tomato sauce. Plan by prepping all the ingredients before you start cooking.

13. Clean with vinegar

If the outer part of your Instant Pot gets a little funky, you can clean it all naturally with vinegar or steam clean it by boiling water and lemon inside. If you have harder water, the vinegar will also break down any mineral deposits that build up and harm your pot. You can wash most of the inner pot and accessories in the dishwasher.

14. Wash most of it in the dishwasher

The inner pot, steam rack and accessories can all be washed in the dishwasher, which makes clean up a breeze! You can just toss the pieces in your dishwasher and go! The lid needs to be hand washed (which isn't too difficult and the outer container can be wiped down by hand after use). Cleaning your Instant Pot after each use will keep it looking great and lasting a very long time.

BEEF & LAMB,PORK RECIPES

Pork Shoulder In Bbq Sauce

Serves:8
Cooking Time: 80 Minutes

Ingredients:
- 4 lb pork shoulder
- 1 tbsp onion powder
- 1 tbsp garlic powder
- Salt and black pepper to taste
- 1 tbsp sweet chili powder
- 2 cups vegetable stock
- For BBQ sauce:
- 6 dates, soaked
- ¼ cup tomato puree
- ½ cup coconut aminos

Directions:
1. In a small bowl, combine onion powder, garlic powder, pepper, salt, and sweet chili powder. Rub the mixture onto the pork. Place the pork in your pressure cooker. Pour the stock around the meat, not over it, and then seal the lid. Select Manual and set the timer to 60 minutes at High. Place all sauce ingredients in a food processor and pulse until smooth. Release the pressure quickly. Grab two forks and shred the meat inside the pot. Pour the sauce over and stir to combine. Serve.

Lamb Cacciatore

Serves:4
Cooking Time: 45 Minutes

Ingredients:

- 1 lb lamb chops
- Salt and black pepper to taste
- 3 tbsp olive oil
- ¼ red bell pepper, sliced
- 1 onion, chopped
- 2 cups mushrooms, sliced
- 2 garlic cloves, minced
- 1 cup dry white wine
- 2 cans (14-oz) tomatoes
- 1 cup chicken stock
- 2 tbsp black olives, pitted
- 1 cup spinach, chopped
- ½ tsp dried oregano

Directions:

1. Season lamb with salt and pepper. Select Sauté and heat oil. Cook lamb for 8 minutes; set aside. Add in bell pepper, onion, and mushrooms. Cook for 7 minutes. Pour in wine and garlic and cook for 2 minutes. Mix in tomatoes, stock, olives, spinach, oregano, and the lamb, along with any juices, Seal the lid, select Manual, and cook for 30 minutes at High. When done, do a natural pressure release for about 10 minutes. Serve.

Orange Cinnamon Ribs

Serves:6
Cooking Time: 70 Minutes

Ingredients:

- 3 lb pork ribs
- ½ cup orange jelly
- 1 cup barbecue sauce
- 1 onion, diced
- 2 tbsp ground cloves
- 1 tbsp brown sugar
- 1 tsp Worcestershire sauce
- 1 tsp ground cinnamon
- 1 tsp rosemary
- Salt and black pepper to taste

Directions:

1. Whisk together all ingredients with ½ cup of water in a bowl. Place ribs in your IP, pour the mixture over, and seal the lid. Set to Manual and cook for 45 minutes at High. Do a natural release, for 10 minutes. Serve hot.

Pork Tenderloin

Serves:5
Cooking Time: 45 Minutes

Ingredients:

- 1 tbsp garlic powder
- 2 tbsp olive oil
- ½ cup soy sauce
- 1 tbsp rosemary
- 2 lb pork tenderloin
- 1 tbsp dry mustard
- Chopped chives for garnish

Directions:

1. Mix all the ingredients with 1 cup of water in a bowl. Heat the olive oil on Sauté and brown the pork on all sides for 5 minutes. Pour in the previously prepared mixture. Seal the lid, select Manual at High, and cook for 20 minutes. When ready, release the pressure naturally for 5 minutes. Serve topped with fresh chives.

Delicious Pork Loin With Turnips & Apples

Serves:4

Cooking Time: 25 Minutes

Ingredients:

- 1 lb pork loin, cut into cubes
- 1 onion, diced
- 2 turnips, peeled and diced
- 1 cup chicken broth
- ½ cup white wine
- 2 apples, diced
- ½ cup sliced leeks
- 1 tbsp vegetable oil
- 1 celery stalk, diced
- 2 tbsp dried parsley
- ¼ tsp thyme
- ½ tsp cumin
- ¼ tsp lemon zest
- Salt and black pepper to taste

Directions:

1. Season the pork with salt and pepper. Heat oil on Sauté. Add pork and cook for a few minutes until browned. Stir in onions and cook for 2 more minutes until soft. Throw in the remaining ingredients, except for the apples. Seal the lid and cook for 15 minutes on Manual at High. When ready, release the pressure quickly. Stir in apples, seal the lid again, and cook at High pressure for another 5 minutes. Do a quick release and serve.

Beef & Tomato Curry

Serves:4
Cooking Time: 48 Minutes

Ingredients:
- 1 lb beef stew meat
- 2 tbsp olive oil
- 4 cups beef broth
- 1 onion, chopped
- 1 can (14.5-oz) tomatoes
- 1 tsp fresh ginger, minced
- 1 jalapeño pepper, chopped
- 1 tbsp curry powder
- Salt and black pepper to taste

Directions:

1. Set your IP to Sauté and heat oil. Season the beef with salt and pepper. Cook for about 5 minutes on both sides until brown; set aside. Sauté curry powder, jalapeño pepper, onion, garlic, and ginger for 3 minutes. Stir in the tomatoes and broth. Seal the lid, select Manual at High, and cook for 20 minutes. When ready, do a quick release. Serve hot.

Pork Shoulder Roast With Noodles

Serves:6

Cooking Time: 51 Minutes

Ingredients:

- 3 lb boneless pork shoulder
- 3 tbsp olive oil
- 2 tbsp oregano
- 6 cups cooked noodles
- 1 cup onion, chopped
- 3 tbsp cornstarch
- 1 cup chicken broth
- Salt and black pepper to taste

Directions:

1. Heat the olive oil on Sauté and brown the pork on all sides for 5-6 minutes. Set aside. Add in the onion and cook for 3 minutes until soften. Return the pork, pour in the broth, and 1 cup of water. Season with salt, pepper, and oregano. Seal the lid, select Manual at High, and cook for 20 minutes. When ready, release the pressure naturally for 10 minutes. Remove the pork from pot and shred it with two forks. In a small bowl, mix the cornstarch with a cup of the cooking liquid and pour in the IP. Cook on Sauté for 2-3 minutes until thickened. Return in the shredded pork and stir. Serve over a bed of noodles.

SNACKS & DESSERTS,APPETIZERS RECIPES

Beef Ribs Texas Bbq Style

Serves:4
Cooking Time: 1 Hour

Ingredients:
- 1 cup BBQ sauce
- 2 tbsp Ancho chili powder
- ½ tbsp garlic powder
- 2 tbsp olive oil
- ½ yellow onion, diced
- 2 lb beef ribs, cut into 2-bone pieces
- Salt and black pepper to taste

Directions:
1. Set your IP to Sauté and heat the olive oil. Rub the beef with salt, pepper, garlic, and chili powder and brown on all the sides for 5-6 minutes. Set aside.
2. To the pot, add the onion and cook for 3 minutes. Return the beef, pour in the BBQ sauce, and a ½ cup of water. Seal lid, select Manual at High, and cook for 45 minutes. When ready, release the pressure naturally for 10 minutes. Serve hot.

Pineapple Chocolate Pudding

Serves:4

Cooking Time: 30 Minutes

Ingredients:

- 1 lime, zested, grated
- ½ cup pineapple juice
- 2 oz chocolate, chopped
- ¼ cup sugar
- 2 tbsp butter, softened
- ¼ cup cornstarch
- 1 cup almond milk
- A pinch of salt
- ½ tsp ginger, caramelized
- 3 eggs, yolks & whites separated

Directions:

1. Combine sugar, cornstarch, salt, and butter in a bowl. Mix in pineapple juice and grated lime zest. Add in the egg yolks, ginger, almond milk, and whisk to mix well. Stir in egg whites. Pour this mixture into custard cups and cover with aluminium foil. Add 1 ½ cups of water to the pressure cooker. Place a trivet into the pressure cooker, and lower the cups onto the rack. Select Manual and cook for 25 minutes at High. Once the cooking is over, do a quick pressure release. Carefully open the lid and stir in the chocolate. Serve chilled.

Almond Butter Lemon Pears

Serves:2

Cooking Time: 10 Minutes

Ingredients:

- 2 pears, cut into wedges
- ½ cup lemon juice
- ½ tsp cinnamon
- 1 tbsp almond butter

Directions:

1. Combine lemon juice and 1 cup of water in the pressure cooker. Place the pear wedges in the steamer basket and lower the basket into the cooker. Seal the lid, select Manual, and cook for 3 minutes at High. Release the pressure quickly. Open the lid and remove the steamer basket. Transfer the pear wedges to a bowl. Drizzle with almond butter and sprinkle with cinnamon.

Duck Legs With Serrano Pepper Sauce

Serves:6

Cooking Time: 40 Minutes

Ingredients:

- 1 ½ lb duck legs
- ½ cup maple syrup
- ½ cup tomato puree
- 2 tsp basil
- 1 tbsp oregano
- 1 tbsp cumin
- Salt and black pepper to taste
- Sauce:
- ½ cup whipping cream
- ½ cup chopped parsley
- ¼ cup olive oil
- 2 tbsp lemon juice
- 2 serrano peppers, chopped
- 1 garlic clove

Directions:

1. Pour 1 ½ cups of water in the pressure cooker and place duck legs in a baking pan. In a bowl, combine all the remaining duck ingredients and pour over the meat. Put the baking pan on top of inserted rack. Seal the lid. Cook on Manual for 20 minutes at High. Release pressure naturally for 10 minutes. Pulse all sauce ingredients in a food processor and transfer to a Serves: bowl. Serve duck bites with the sauce.

Mayonnaise & Bacon Stuffed Eggs

Serves:4

Cooking Time: 23 Minutes

Ingredients:

- 8 eggs
- 2 oz fried bacon, chopped
- Salt and black pepper to taste
- 1 tsp mayonnaise
- Chopped chives for garnish

Directions:

1. Place eggs into the IP and cover with water. Seal the lid and press Manual. Cook at High for 8 minutes. After cooking, do a quick pressure release. Remove eggs and carefully put them in a bowl of ice water for 5 minutes. Peel off the eggshells. Cut eggs in half and remove the yolks. In a bowl, mix egg yolks, mayo, salt, pepper, and fried bacon. Stir to combine well. Fill the egg white with egg yolk mixture, top with chives for garnish.

Cauliflower Popcorn

Serves:6

Cooking Time: 15 Minutes

Ingredients:

- 10 oz cauliflower, florets
- 1 tbsp olive oil
- Salt and black pepper to taste

Directions:

1. In a bowl, sprinkle florets with salt and olive oil. Add 1 cup of water into the IP. Place trivet inside. Put florets in a baking pan and place on top of the trivet. Seal the lid and press Manual. Cook for 5 minutes at High. After cooking, do a quick pressure release. Serve.

Fall Root Vegetable Mix

Serves:4

Cooking Time: 25 Minutes

Ingredients:

- 1 ½ lb mixed root vegetables
- 3 garlic cloves, minced
- 1 onion, sliced
- 1 cup vegetable broth
- 2 tbsp olive oil
- A pinch of salt
- 2 tbsp parsley, chopped

Directions:

1. Heat olive oil on Sauté in the IP and cook onion and garlic for 3 minutes. Cut all the root vegetables into small pieces, and add them to the cooker along with salt and broth. Seal the lid, press Manual, and cook for 7 minutes at High. After cooking, do a quick pressure release. Serve hot sprinkled with parsley.

VEGETABLE & VEGETARIAN RECIPES

Spicy Red Lentils With Yogurt

Serves:4

Cooking Time: 20 Minutes

Ingredients:

- 1 cup red lentils
- 3 tsp olive oil
- Salt and black pepper to taste
- 1 tsp ground turmeric
- 1 tbsp cumin seeds
- ½ tsp cayenne pepper
- ½ tsp ground bay leaves
- 1 tsp parsley
- Fresh cilantro to garnish
- Yogurt to garnish
- 1 sliced jalapeño, to garnish

Directions:

1. Put all ingredients in the cooker, pour in 3 cups of water, and seal the lid. Cook for 10 minutes on Manual at High. Do a quick pressure release. Serve garnished with fresh cilantro, jalapeño slices, and yogurt.

Kohlsuppe Traditional German Cabbage Soup

Serves: 4

Cooking Time: 20 Minutes

Ingredients:

- 2 teaspoons chicken schmaltz
- 1 pound smoked sausage, sliced
- 1 onion, chopped
- 2 garlic cloves, minced
- 2 carrots, chopped
- 1 celery stalk, chopped
- 2 fresh tomatoes, chopped
- 4 cups chicken broth
- 1/2 teaspoon basil
- 1/2 teaspoon dried thyme
- 1/2 teaspoon dried oregano
- 1 teaspoon paprika
- 1 pound cabbage, cored and shredded
- Salt and ground black pepper, to taste

Directions:

1. Press the "Sauté" button and melt the chicken schmaltz. Then, cook the sausage and onion for about 3 minutes. Now, stir in the garlic and continue to sauté for 30 seconds more, stirring frequently.
2. Add the remaining ingredients; stir to combine.
3. Secure the lid. Choose the "Manual" mode and cook for 10 minutes at High pressure. Once cooking is complete, use a quick pressure release; carefully remove the lid.
4. Serve in individual bowls. Bon appétit!

Parsnip & Cauliflower Mash With Chives

Serves: 8

Cooking Time: 15 Minutes

Ingredients:

- 1 ½ lb parsnips, peeled and cubed
- 1 head cauliflower, cut into florets
- 2 garlic cloves
- Salt and black pepper to taste
- 2 cups water
- ¼ cup sour cream
- ¼ cup grated Parmesan cheese
- 1 tbsp butter
- 2 tbsp minced chives

Directions:

1. In the pot, mix parsnips, garlic, water, salt, cauliflower, and pepper. Seal the lid and cook on High Pressure for 4 minutes. Release the pressure quickly. Drain parsnips and cauliflower and return to pot.
2. Add Parmesan, butter, and sour cream. Use a potato masher to mash until desired consistency is attained. Into the mashed parsnip, add 1 tbsp chives; place to a serving plate and garnish with remaining chives.

Creamy Potatoes

Serves: 4
Cooking Time: 25 Minutes

Ingredients:

- 6 potatoes, sliced
- 1 tsp scallions
- 2 tbsp butter
- Salt and black pepper to taste
- 1 cup chicken broth
- ¼ cup buttermilk
- ¼ cup milk
- 2 tbsp potato starch
- ¼ tsp cayenne pepper

Directions:

1. Place the potatoes and broth in your Instant Pot and seal the lid. Select Manual and cook for 5 minutes on High. Once ready, perform a quick pressure release and unlock the lid. Remove potatoes to a greased baking sheet.
2. Select Sauté on the pot and mix in the remaining cooking liquid with buttermilk, butter, milk, scallions, and potato starch and cook for 2-3 minutes until the sauce thickens. Pour it over the potatoes and place under the broiler for about 4 minutes. Sprinkle with cayenne pepper and serve immediately.

Low-carb Eggplant Lasagna

Serves: 2-4

Cooking Time: 35 Minutes

Ingredients:

- 1 large eggplant, chopped
- 4 oz mozzarella, chopped
- 3 oz mascarpone cheese, at room temperature
- 2 tomatoes, chopped
- ¼ cup olive oil
- 1 tsp salt
- ½ tsp ground black pepper
- 1 tsp oregano, dried

Directions:

1. Grease a baking dish with olive oil. Slice the eggplant and make a layer in the dish. Cover with mozzarella and tomato slices. Top with mascarpone cheese. Repeat the process until you run out of ingredients.
2. In a bowl, mix olive oil, salt, pepper, and dried oregano. Pour the mixture over the lasagna, and add ½ cup of water. In your inner pot, Pour 1 ½ cups of water and insert a trivet.
3. Lower the baking dish on the trivet, Seal the lid and cook on High Pressure for 4 minutes. When ready, do a natural release, for 10 minutes.

Cauliflower Mash Dish

Serves: 2-4

Cooking Time: 20 Minutes

Ingredients:

- 1½ cups water
- 1 cauliflower, florets separated
- Salt and ground black pepper to taste
- 1 tbsp butter
- ½ tsp turmeric
- 2 chives, finely chopped

Directions:

1. Prepare the Instant Pot by adding the water to the pot and placing the steamer basket in it.
2. Put the cauliflower in the basket. Close and lock the lid.
3. Select MANUAL and cook at HIGH pressure for 6 minutes.
4. Once cooking is complete, let the pressure Release Naturally for 2 minutes. Release any remaining steam manually. Uncover the pot.
5. Using a potato masher or fork, mash the cauliflower.
6. Season with salt and pepper. Add in the butter and turmeric and mix well.
7. Top with chopped chives and serve.

Vegetable Bowl With Tahini Sauce

Serves: 4

Cooking Time: 10 Minutes

Ingredients:

- 4 carrots, sliced
- 4 medium potatoes, diced
- 1 pound cauliflower florets
- 2 tablespoons olive oil
- 1/2 teaspoon sea salt
- 1 cup vegetable broth
- 1/3 cup tahini
- 1/4 cup olive oil
- 1/3 cup water
- 1 clove garlic, pressed
- 2 tablespoons fresh lime juice
- 1 tablespoon fresh parsley, finely chopped

Directions:

1. Place the vegetables, olive oil, salt, and vegetable broth in the inner pot of your Instant Pot.
2. Secure the lid. Choose the "Manual" mode and cook for 4 minutes at High pressure. Once cooking is complete, use a quick pressure release; carefully remove the lid.
3. Meanwhile, make the tahini sauce by mixing the remaining ingredients. Serve the warm vegetables with the tahini sauce on the side. Bon appétit!

POULTRY RECIPES

Colorful Vegetable & Chicken Risotto

Serves: 4
Cooking Time: 65 Minutes

Ingredients:

- 10 oz chicken breasts, boneless, skinless, cut into pieces
- 1 cup rice
- 6 oz button mushrooms, stems removed
- 1 red bell pepper, halved, seeds removed
- 1 green bell pepper, halved, seeds removed
- 1 yellow bell pepper, halved, seeds removed
- 6 oz broccoli, cut into florets
- ½ cup sweet corn
- 2 carrots, peeled and chopped
- 2 tbsp olive oil
- 1 tbsp butter
- Salt and black pepper to taste
- 1 tsp fresh basil, finely chopped
- Parmesan cheese for topping

Directions:

1. Add rice and pour in 3 cups of water. Stir in butter, pepper and salt and seal the lid. Cook on Rice mode for 8 minutes on High. Do a quick release and remove the rice.
2. Heat oil on Sauté, and add carrots and broccoli. Sauté for 10 minutes. Add sweet corn and bell peppers and cook for 5 minutes, stirring constantly. Finally, stir in mushrooms, and cook for 3-4 minutes.
3. Remove the vegetables, mix with rice and set aside. Add the chicken to the pot and pour in 2 cups of water. Season with salt and pepper. Seal the lid and cook on High pressure for 7 minutes. Do a quick release. Open the lid, stir in rice and vegetables and serve warm sprinkled with Parmesan cheese and fresh basil.

Chicken & Leek Casserole With Sausage

Serves:5
Cooking Time: 35 Minutes

Ingredients:
- 1 tsp garlic, minced
- 1 cup onions, chopped
- 1 lb sausages, sliced
- 4 chicken thighs
- 3 tbsp olive oil
- 2 cups chicken stock
- 3 cups leeks, chopped
- 1 tsp paprika
- Salt and black pepper to taste
- 2 jalapenos, chopped
- 26 oz canned tomatoes, chopped
- 1 ½ cups canned kidney beans

Directions:
1. On Sauté, heat the oil and brown the sausages for about 5 minutes per side. Transfer to a large bowl. In the same oil, add the thighs and brown them for 5 minutes. Remove to the same bowl as the sausages. To the cooker, stir in onions and jalapeños. Cook for 3 minutes. Add in garlic and cook for 1 minute. Stir in tomatoes, beans, stock, leeks, paprika, salt, and pepper. Return the reserved sausage and thighs, and stir well. Seal the lid and cook for 10 minutes on Manual at High. When ready, do a quick release and serve hot.

Ground Turkey Casserole

Serves: 4

Cooking Time:20 Minutes

Ingredients:

- 1 ½ pounds ground turkey
- Salt and ground black pepper, to taste
- 2 ripe tomatoes, pureed
- 1 red chili pepper, minced
- 3 garlic cloves, smashed
- 2 tablespoons fresh parsley, roughly chopped
- 1 bay leaf
- 1 yellow onion, chopped
- 1 (1 ½-pound) head of cabbage, shredded
- 1 tablespoon lard
- 1 sweet pepper, sliced

Directions:

1. Press the "Sauté" button and melt the lard. Now, brown the ground turkey until no longer pink, about 3 minutes.
2. Add the remaining ingredients and secure the lid.
3. Secure the lid. Choose the "Manual" mode and cook for 10 minutes at High pressure. Once cooking is complete, use a natural pressure release; carefully remove the lid.
4. Divide between individual bowls and serve warm. Enjoy!

Chicken Wings And Scallions And Tomato Sauce

Serves:4

Cooking Time: 25 Minutes

Ingredients:

- 1 tbsp. olive oil
- 6 scallions, chopped
- A pinch of salt and black pepper
- 8 chicken wings
- 8 oz. tomato sauce
- 2 cups chicken stock
- 1 tomato, chopped

Directions:

1. Set your Instant Pot to Sauté and heat the olive oil.
2. Add the scallions, salt, and pepper and sauté for 5 minutes, stirring occasionally.
3. Stir in the chicken wings and cook for 5 minutes until lightly browned. Add the remaining ingredients to the pot and stir well.
4. Lock the lid. Select the Manual mode and set the cooking time for 15 minutes at High Pressure.
5. Once cooking is complete, do a natural pressure release for 10 minutes, then release any remaining pressure. Carefully open the lid.
6. Remove from the pot to a plate and serve hot.

Chili Lime Chicken

Serves: 8
Cooking Time: 15 Minutes

Ingredients:

- 2 pounds chicken breasts, bones removed
- Juice of 2 medium limes
- 1 ½ teaspoons chili powder
- 1 teaspoon cumin
- 1 teaspoon onion powder
- 6 cloves garlic, minced
- ½ teaspoon liquid smoke
- Salt and pepper

Directions:

1. Place all ingredients in the Instant Pot.
2. Give a good stir.
3. Close the lid and press the Manual button.4. Adjust the cooking time to 15 minutes.
4. Do quick pressure release.

Easy Primavera Chicken Stew

Serves: 4
Cooking Time: 55 Minutes

Ingredients:

- 4 green onions, chopped
- 3 garlic cloves, peeled and crushed
- 3 new potatoes, peeled and chopped
- 8 baby carrots, chopped
- 4 oz can tomato sauce
- 1 tsp salt
- 8 oz chicken breast, cut into bite-sized pieces
- 2 cups chicken broth
- 2 tbsp olive oil

Directions:

1. Place the veggies in the instant pot and pour enough water to cover. Seal the lid and cook on Manual/Pressure Cook for 15 minutes on High. Do a quick release. Remove the vegetables along with the liquid.
2. Heat oil on Sauté and stir-fry the vegetables for 5 minutes. Add the remaining ingredients and seal the lid. Set on Poultry and cook for 15 minutes on High. Do a natural release, for 10 minutes and serve hot.

Chicken With Artichokes And Bacon

Serves:4

Cooking Time: 25 Minutes

Ingredients:

- 2 chicken breasts, skinless, boneless, and halved
- 2 cups canned artichokes, drained, and chopped
- 1 cup bacon, cooked and crumbled
- 1 cup water
- 2 tbsps. tomato paste
- 1 tbsp. chives, chopped
- Salt, to taste

Directions:

1. Mix all the ingredients in your Instant Pot until well combined.
2. Lock the lid. Select the Poultry mode and set the cooking time for 25 minutes at High Pressure.
3. Once cooking is complete, do a natural pressure release for 10 minutes, then release any remaining pressure. Carefully open the lid.
4. Remove from the pot to a large plate and serve.

PASTA & RICE RECIPES

Chicken, Broccoli And Rice Casserole

Serves: 4
Cooking Time: 30 Minutes

Ingredients:
- 3 tablespoons butter, melted
- 1 chicken breast, skinless
- 1 shallot, sliced
- 1 teaspoon garlic, minced
- 1 pound broccoli florets
- 1 cup white rice
- 1 cup tomato puree
- 2 cups chicken broth
- 1 teaspoon paprika
- 1 teaspoon Italian seasoning blend
- Kosher salt and freshly ground pepper, to taste
- 5 ounces cheddar cheese, shredded

Directions:
1. Press the "Sauté" button and melt 1 tablespoon of butter. Once hot, cook the chicken breast until it is golden brown on both sides.
2. Shred the chicken with two forks. Add it back to the inner pot. Add the shallots, garlic, broccoli, rice, tomato puree, and chicken broth; stir in the remaining butter.
3. Season with the paprika, Italian seasonings, salt, and black pepper.
4. Secure the lid. Choose the "Rice" mode and cook for 10 minutes at Low pressure. Once cooking is complete, use a natural pressure release for 10 minutes; carefully remove the lid.
5. Top with cheese. Seal the lid again and let it sit in the residual heat until the cheese melts. Serve immediately.

Butternut Squash & Cheese Risotto

Serves: 4

Cooking Time: 20 Minutes

Ingredients:

- ½ pound butternut squash, cubed
- 3 tbsp olive oil
- 2 cloves garlic, minced
- 1 yellow onion, chopped
- 2 cups arborio rice
- 4 cups chicken stock
- ½ cup pumpkin puree
- 1 tsp thyme, chopped
- ½ tsp nutmeg
- ½ tsp ginger, grated
- ½ tsp cinnamon
- ½ cup heavy cream
- Salt and black pepper to taste
- ¼ cup shaved Parmesan cheese

Directions:

1. Preheat the oven to 360°F. Spread the squash cubes on a baking tray and drizzle with olive oil. Roast for 20 minutes until tender. Warm oil in your Instant Pot on Sauté and add garlic and onion; cook for 3 minutes. Stir in rice, stock, pumpkin puree, thyme, nutmeg, ginger, and cinnamon. Seal the lid, select Manual, and cook for 10 minutes on High.
2. When done, perform a quick pressure release and unlock the lid. Mix in heavy cream, salt, and pepper. Top with pumpkin cubes and Parmesan shaves and serve.

Coconut Rice Breakfast

Serves: 4

Cooking Time: 25 Minutes

Ingredients:

- 1 cup brown rice
- 1 cup water
- 1 cup coconut milk
- ½ cup coconut chips
- ¼ cup walnuts, chopped
- ¼ cup raisins
- A pinch of cinnamon powder
- ½ cup maple syrup

Directions:

1. Place the rice and water in your Instant Pot. Seal the lid, select Manual, and cook for 15 minutes on High pressure. When ready, perform a quick pressure release and unlock the lid. Stir in coconut milk, coconut chips, raisins, cinnamon, and maple syrup.
2. Seal the lid, select Manual, and cook for another 5 minutes on High pressure. When over, perform a quick pressure release and unlock the lid. Top with walnuts and serve.

Kiwi Steel Cut Oatmeal

Serves: 4

Cooking Time: 25 Minutes

Ingredients:

- 2 kiwi, mashed
- 2 cups steel cut oatmeal
- 3 cups water
- ¼ tsp nutmeg
- 1 tsp cinnamon
- 1 tsp vanilla
- ¼ tsp salt
- ½ cup hazelnuts, chopped
- ¼ cup honey

Directions:

1. Place the kiwi, oats, water, nutmeg, cinnamon, vanilla, and salt in your Instant Pot and stir to combine. Seal the lid and cook on Manual for 10 minutes on High pressure. When done, allow a natural release for 10 minutes and unlock the lid. Mix in hazelnuts and honey and let chill. Serve.

Sausage & Spinach Rigatoni

Serves: 2-4

Cooking Time: 45 Minutes

Ingredients:

- 1 tbsp butter
- ½ cup diced red bell pepper
- 1 onion, chopped
- 3 cups vegetable broth
- ¼ cup tomato purée
- 4 sausage links, chopped
- ½ cup milk
- 2 tsp chili powder
- salt and ground black pepper to taste
- 12 ounces rigatoni pasta
- 1 cup baby spinach
- ½ cup Parmesan cheese

Directions:

1. Warm butter on Sauté. Add red bell pepper, onion, and sausage, and cook for 5 minutes. Mix in broth, chili, tomato paste, salt, and pepper. Stir in rigatoni pasta.
2. Seal the lid and cook on High Pressure for 12 minutes. Naturally release Pressure for 20 minutes. Stir in spinach and let simmer until wilted. Sprinkle with Parmesan and serve.

Smoked Salmon And Green Bean Pilau

Serves: 4
Cooking Time:20 Minutes

Ingredients:

- 1 cup white rice
- 1 pound smoked salmon steak
- 4 ounces green beans
- 1 cup vegetable broth
- 1 onion, chopped
- 2 cloves garlic, minced
- 1/2 cup milk
- Sea salt and ground black pepper, to season
- 1 tablespoon butter

Directions:

1. Press the "Sauté" button and melt the butter. When the butter starts to sizzle, add the onion; sauté the onion until just tender and fragrant.
2. Now, stir in the garlic and continue to sauté an additional minute or until fragrant.
3. Add the rice, broth, milk, salmon, and green beans; season with salt and black pepper.
4. Secure the lid. Choose the "Manual" mode and cook for 4 minutes at High pressure. Once cooking is complete, use a natural pressure release for 10 minutes; carefully remove the lid. Bon appétit!

Cheesy Macaroni With Chicken & Bacon

Serves: 2-4

Cooking Time: 35 Minutes

Ingredients:

- 4 bacon slices, chopped
- 2 tbsp olive oil
- 4 chicken breasts
- 1 tbsp ranch dressing mix
- 16 oz macaroni
- 3 cups chicken broth
- Salt and black pepper to taste
- 4 oz cream cheese, softened
- 1 cup grated Monterey Jack cheese

Directions:

1. Set your Instant Pot to Sauté and adjust to medium heat. Cook bacon in inner pot until brown and crispy. Remove onto a plate and set aside. Heat olive oil in bacon fat, season chicken with ranch dressing mix, and sear in oil until golden, 5 minutes. Return bacon to pot and top with macaroni and chicken broth. Season with salt and pepper.
2. Seal the lid, select Manual/Pressure Cook on High, and set cooking time to 6 minutes. After cooking, perform a quick pressure release to let out remaining steam, and unlock the lid. Select Sauté and mix in cream cheese and Monterey Jack cheese until melted, 3 minutes. Dish food and serve warm.

BRUNCH & SIDE DISHES RECIPES

Tasty Asparagus Soup

Serves: 4
Cooking Time: 40 Minutes

Ingredients:
- 2 lb fresh asparagus, trimmed
- 2 onions, chopped
- 1 cup heavy cream
- 4 cups vegetable broth
- 2 tbsp butter
- 1 tbsp vegetable oil
- ½ tsp salt
- ½ tsp dried oregano
- ½ tsp paprika

Directions:
1. Melt butter on Sauté, and add 1 tbsp of oil. Stir-fry the onions for 2 minutes, until translucent. Add asparagus, oregano, salt, and paprika. Stir well and cook until asparagus soften, for a few minutes.
2. Pour the broth and mix well to combine. Seal the lid and cook on Soup/Broth for 20 minutes on High. Do a quick release and whisk in 1 cup of heavy cream. Serve chilled or warm.

Ham, Egg, And Cheese Casserole

Serves: 8

Cooking Time: 15 Minutes

Ingredients:

- 1 package hash browns, cubed
- 1 large onion, diced
- 2 cups ham, chopped
- 2 cups cheddar cheese, grated
- 10 large eggs, beaten
- 1 cup whole milk
- Salt and pepper to taste

Directions:

1. Spray the inside of the Instant Pot with cooking spray.2. Place the hash browns at the bottom.
2. Arrange half of the onion, ham, and cheese. Repeat the process until all ingredients are layered into the pot.
3. In a mixing bowl, combine the eggs and milk. Season with salt and pepper.5. Pour over the milk mixture on top of the layered ingredients.
4. Close the lid and seal off the vent.
5. Press the Manual button and cook on high for 15 minutes.
6. Do natural pressure release.

Carrot & Nut Cakes

Serves:8
Cooking Time: 25 Minutes

Ingredients:

- ¼ cup coconut oil
- ½ cup milk
- ½ cup walnuts, chopped
- 1 tsp apple pie spice
- 1 cup carrots, shredded
- 3 eggs
- ½ cup applesauce
- 1 cup ground hazelnuts

Directions:

1. Pour 1 cup water into your Instant Pot and fit in a trivet. Place coconut oil, milk, eggs, applesauce, hazelnuts, and apple pie spice, in a large bowl. Beat the mixture well with an electric mixer until it becomes fluffy.
2. Fold in the carrots and walnuts. Pour the batter into silicone muffin cups and arrange them on the trivet. Seal the lid, and cook on Manual at High for 15 minutes. When ready, do a quick pressure release. Remove the muffins, and cool for a few minutes before serving.

Parsley Creamy Tomato Soup

Serves: 4
Cooking Time: 45 Minutes

Ingredients:

- 2 lb tomatoes, diced
- 1 cup white beans, pre-cooked
- 1 small onion, diced
- 2 garlic cloves, crushed
- 1 cup heavy cream
- 1 cup vegetable broth
- 2 tbsp fresh parsley, finely chopped
- Salt and black pepper to taste
- 2 tbsp olive oil
- ½ tsp sugar

Directions:

1. Warm oil on Sauté mode. Stir-fry onion and garlic on Sauté, for 2 minutes. Add tomatoes, beans, broth, 3 cups of water, parsley, salt, pepper, and a little bit of sugar to balance the bitterness.
2. Seal the lid and cook on Soup/Broth for 30 minutes on High Pressure. Release the pressure naturally, for 10 minutes.
3. Top with a dollop of heavy cream and chopped parsley, to serve.

Authentic German Salad With Smoked Bacon

Serves: 6

Cooking Time: 20 Minutes

Ingredients:

- 6 slices smoked bacon, chopped
- ½ cup apple cider vinegar
- ½ cup water
- 3 tbsp sugar
- 2 tsp mustard
- Salt and black pepper to serve
- 6 red potatoes, peeled and quartered
- 2 red onions, chopped
- A handful of parsley for garnishing

Directions:

1. On Sauté, briefly brown the bacon for 2 minutes per side. Set aside. In a bowl, mix sugar, salt, mustard, vinegar, water, and black pepper. In the pot, add potatoes, chopped bacon, and onions, and top with the vinegar mixture.
2. Seal the lid and cook for 6 minutes on High Pressure. Release pressure naturally for 10 minutes. Place on serving plate and add fresh parsley for garnishing.

Black Bean And Egg Casserole

Serves: 3

Cooking Time: 20 Minutes

Ingredients:

- 4 large eggs, well-beaten
- ½ lb. mild ground sausage
- ¼ large red onion, chopped
- ½ red bell pepper, chopped
- ½ can black beans, rinsed
- ¼ cup green onions
- ¼ cup flour
- ½ cup Cotija cheese*
- ½ cup mozzarella cheese
- Sour cream, cilantro to garnish

Directions:

1. Add the sausage and onion to the Instant Pot and select the "Sauté" function and cook for 3 minutes.
2. Combine flour with eggs and add this mixture to the sausages.
3. Add all the vegetables, cheeses, and beans.
4. Secure the lid of the cooker and press the "Manual" function key.
5. Adjust the time to 20 minutes and cook at high pressure.
6. After the beep, release the pressure naturally and remove the lid.
7. Remove the inner pot, place a plate on top then flip the pot to transfer the casserole to the plate.
8. Serve warm.

Power Swiss Chard & Spinach Omelet

Serves: 2

Cooking Time: 20 Minutes

Ingredients:

- 1 cup spinach, chopped
- 1 cup Swiss chard, chopped
- 4 eggs
- 2 tbsp olive oil
- ½ tsp salt
- ¼ tsp red pepper flakes

Directions:

1. Grease the inner pot with olive oil. Stir-fry the Swiss chard and spinach for 5 minutes on Sauté. Set aside. Whisk the eggs, salt, and red pepper flakes. Pour the mixture in the pot. Spread the eggs with a wooden spatula and cook for 3-4 minutes on Sauté. With a spatula, ease around the edges and slide to a serving plate. Add Swiss chard and spinach and fold it over in half.

STOCKS AND SAUCES

Ragù Alla Bolognese

Serves: 4

Cooking Time: 30 Minutes

Ingredients:

- ½ tbsp butter
- 1 small onion, chopped
- 2 garlic cloves, minced
- 1 carrot, chopped
- 1 celery stalk, chopped
- 1 lb ground beef
- ¼ cup red wine
- 1 cup tomato sauce
- 1 tbsp sugar
- Salt and black pepper to taste
- ¼ tsp basil
- ¼ cup half and half
- ¼ cup parsley, chopped

Directions:

1. Melt the butter in your Instant Pot on Sauté. Add in onion, garlic, celery, and carrot and cook for 4-5 minutes until tender. Stir in ground beef and brown for 4-5 minutes, stirring periodically. Pour in tomato sauce, red wine, sugar, salt, pepper, and basil and seal the lid. Select Manual and cook for 15 minutes on High.
2. When over, allow a natural release for 10 minutes, then perform a quick pressure release, and unlock the lid. Stir in half and half and top with parsley. Serve immediately.

Tasty Beef Neck Bone Stock

Serves: 8

Cooking Time: 2 Hours 10 Minutes

Ingredients:
- 1 carrot, chopped
- 2 onions, chopped
- 2 cups celery, chopped
- 2 pounds beef neck bones
- 12 cups water, or more
- 1 tsp cider vinegar
- 2 bay leaves
- 10 peppercorns
- Salt to taste

Directions:
1. Add carrot, peppercorns, salt, bay leaves, celery, vinegar, onions, and beef bones. Add enough water to cover ingredients. Seal the lid and cook on High Pressure for 120 minutes. Release pressure naturally for about 20 minutes.
2. Remove the bones and bay leaves, and discard. Use a fine-mesh strainer to strain the liquid. Allow the broth to cool. From the surface, skim fat and throw away. Refrigerate for a maximum of 7 days.

Easy Onion Gravy

Serves: 4
Cooking Time: 10 Minutes

Ingredients:

- 1 onion, chopped
- 1 tsp onion powder
- 3 cups vegetable broth
- 2 cups cream cheese
- 2 tsp dried parsley, chopped
- 1 tbsp olive oil

Directions:

1. Heat oil on Sauté, and stir-fry the onion for 5 minutes, or until translucent.
2. Stir in the remaining ingredients. Seal the lid and cook on High Pressure for 5 minutes. Do a quick Pressure release and serve immediately.

Beef Broth With Vermicelli Egg Noodles

Serves: 6

Cooking Time: 80 Minutes

Ingredients:

- 2 lb beef bones
- 2 carrots, cut into large chunks
- 3 celery stalks, chopped
- 1 onion, quartered
- 2 garlic cloves, minced
- 2 bay leaves
- 2 tbsp whole black peppercorns
- Salt to taste
- ½ cup vermicelli egg noddles
- 1 habanero pepper, sliced
- 2 green onions, sliced

Directions:

1. Place the beef bones, carrots, celery, onion, garlic, bay leaves, black peppercorns, salt, and 6 cups of water in your Instant Pot and seal the lid. Select Manual and cook for 60 minutes on High. Once over, allow a natural release for 10 minutes and unlock the lid. Strain the broth through a fine-mesh sieve, discard the solids, and return to the pot.
2. Press Sauté and add in the vermicelli noddles; cook for 4-5 minutes until tender. Ladle the broth into bowla and top with habanero pepper and green onions to serve.

Instant Pot Strawberry Applesauce

Serves: 6
Cooking Time: 5 Minutes

Ingredients:

- 8 peeled apples, cored and sliced
- 3 cups strawberries, hulled and chopped
- ¼ teaspoon cinnamon powder
- 2 tablespoons lemon juice

Directions:

1. Place all ingredients in the Instant Pot.
2. Close the lid and press the Manual button.
3. Adjust the cooking time to 5 minutes
4. Do natural pressure release.
5. Place in mason jars.

Instant Pot Herb Stock

Serves: 4
Cooking Time: 15 Minutes

Ingredients:
- A handful of rosemary,
- 1 sprig of parsley
- 3 bay leaves
- 2 cloves of garlic, crushed
- 1 teaspoon black peppercorns
- 4 cups water

Directions:
1. Place all ingredients in the Instant Pot.
2. Close the lid and press the Manual button.
3. Adjust the cooking time to 15 minutes
4. Do natural pressure release.
5. Run the stock through a sieve and discard the solids.
6. Place in mason jars and store in the fridge until ready to serve.

Eggplant Light Sauce With Wine

Serves: 6

Cooking Time: 10 Minutes

Ingredients:

- 2 tablespoons olive oil
- 1 pound eggplants, sliced
- 4 garlic cloves, minced
- 2 tomatoes, chopped
- 1 cup white wine
- 1 teaspoon oregano
- 1/2 teaspoon rosemary
- 1 teaspoon basil
- Sea salt and ground black pepper, to taste
- 2 tablespoons tahini (sesame butter
- 1/2 cup Romano cheese, freshly grated

Directions:

1. Press the "Sauté" button and heat the olive oil. Then, cook the eggplant slices until they are charred at the bottom. Work with batches.
2. Add the garlic, tomatoes, wine, and spices.
3. Secure the lid. Choose the "Bean/Chili" mode and cook for 3 minutes at High pressure. Once cooking is complete, use a quick pressure release; carefully remove the lid.
4. Press the "Sauté" button again to thicken the cooking liquid. Add the tahini paste and stir to combine. Top with Romano cheese and serve.

LOW CARB RECIPES

Italian Keto Balls With Marinara Sauce

Serves: 6

Cooking Time:15 Minutes

Ingredients:

- 1 ½ cups Romano cheese, grated
- Sea salt and ground black pepper, to your liking
- 2 cloves garlic, finely chopped
- 2 tablespoons fresh parsley, chopped
- 1 tablespoon olive oil
- 8 eggs, whisked
- 1 cup pork rinds, crushed
- 1 ½ cups low-carb marinara sauce

Directions:

1. Press the "Sauté" button to heat up the Instant Pot. Add the marinara sauce and bring it to a boil.
2. Now, in a mixing bowl, thoroughly combine the remaining ingredients. Form the mixture into balls.
3. Then, drop the balls into the hot marinara sauce.
4. Secure the lid. Choose "Manual" mode and High pressure; cook for 8 minutes. Once cooking is complete, use a quick pressure release; carefully remove the lid. Bon appétit!

Ground Meat And Cheese-stuffed Peppers

Serves: 4

Cooking Time:25 Minutes

Ingredients:

- 1 cup Cotija cheese, grated
- 4 eggs, whisked
- 1 (1-ounce) package taco seasoning mix
- 4 bell peppers, remove seeds and cut the tops off
- 8 ounces canned tomato sauce
- 2 garlic cloves, minced
- 1/2 cup onion, chopped
- 1/2 pound ground beef
- 1/4 pound ground pork
- Salt and ground black pepper, to taste

Directions:

1. Start by adding 1 cup of water and a metal rack to the bottom of the Instant Pot. Spritz a casserole dish with a nonstick cooking spray.
2. In a mixing bowl, thoroughly combine the ground meat, eggs, garlic, onion, salt, pepper, taco seasoning mix, and Cotija cheese.
3. Fill the peppers with the cheese/meat mixture. Place the peppers on the rack in the Instant Pot. Pour the tomato sauce over the peppers.
4. Secure the lid. Choose "Manual" mode and High pressure; cook for 20 minutes. Once cooking is complete, use a natural pressure release; carefully remove the lid. Bon appétit!

Dijon Mustard-herb Chicken

Serves: 4
Cooking Time:20 Minutes

Ingredients:
- 1 tablespoon Dijon mustard
- 1 pound chicken breasts, boneless
- 1 teaspoon garlic powder
- 1/2 teaspoon dried sage
- 1/2 cup heavy cream
- 1 teaspoon paprika
- 1 cup chicken bone broth
- 1 teaspoon dried basil
- 1/2 teaspoon dried oregano
- 2 tablespoons olive oil, divided
- Sea salt and ground black pepper, to taste

Directions:
1. Press the "Sauté" button and heat the olive oil. Sear the chicken breasts until they are no longer pink.
2. Add the seasonings, mustard, and chicken bone broth.
3. Secure the lid. Choose "Manual" mode and cook for 8 minutes at High pressure. Once cooking is complete, use a natural pressure release; carefully remove the lid.
4. Lastly, add the heavy cream, cover with the lid, and let it sit in the residual heat for 6 to 8 minutes. Serve in individual bowls. Enjoy!

Cod Fish, Herb And Tomato Chowder

Serves: 4

Cooking Time:12 Minutes

Ingredients:

- 1 onion, chopped
- 1/4 teaspoon hot sauce
- 1/2 teaspoon paprika
- 2 garlic cloves, minced
- 1/2 teaspoon dried dill weed
- 1/4 cup cooking wine
- 1 pound cod fish, cut into bite-sized pieces
- 1/2 teaspoon basil
- 2 ripe tomatoes, pureed
- 2 tablespoons tomato paste
- 1/4 teaspoon dried oregano
- 1/2 stick butter, at room temperature
- 1 cup shellfish stock
- Sea salt and freshly ground black pepper, to taste

Directions:

1. Press the "Sauté" button and melt the butter; once hot, cook the onion and garlic for about 2 minutes or until they are just tender.
2. Add the remaining ingredients.
3. Secure the lid. Choose the "Manual" mode and cook for 5 minutes at High pressure. Once cooking is complete, use a quick pressure release; carefully remove the lid.
4. Ladle into serving bowls and serve immediately.

Festive Herb Chicken

Serves: 4

Cooking Time:35 Minutes

Ingredients:

- 1 (3 ½ pounds) whole chicken
- Salt and ground black pepper, to taste
- 1 tablespoon paprika
- 4 tablespoons butter, softened
- 1 head of garlic, crushed
- 2 quarts water
- 2 rosemary sprigs, crushed
- 2 thyme sprigs, crushed

Directions:

1. In a small mixing dish, thoroughly combine the butter, garlic, salt, black pepper, paprika, rosemary, and thyme.
2. Pour the water into the inner pot.
3. Pat the chicken dry. Then, rub the butter mixture all over the chicken to season well. Place the chicken in the inner pot.
4. Secure the lid. Choose "Manual" mode. Cook for 20 minutes at High pressure. Once cooking is complete, use a natural pressure release; carefully remove the lid.
5. Afterwards, place the chicken under the broiler for 10 minutes until the skin is lightly crisped. Bon appétit!

Two-cheese Cauliflower Muffins

Serves: 6
Cooking Time:15 Minutes

Ingredients:

- 1/2 cup Cotija cheese, grated
- 1 cup Romano cheese, preferably freshly grated
- 1/4 teaspoon dried oregano
- 2 garlic cloves, minced
- 1/2 cup scallions, chopped
- 1/2 teaspoon dried dill weed
- 1/2 teaspoon dried basil
- Salt and ground black pepper, to taste
- 7 eggs, beaten
- 1/2 pound cauliflower, riced
- Sea salt and ground black pepper, to taste
- 1/2 teaspoon cayenne pepper
- 2 tablespoons olive oil

Directions:

1. Start by adding 1 ½ cups of water and a metal rack to the bottom of the Instant Pot. Spritz each muffin cup with a nonstick cooking spray.
2. Mix the ingredients until everything is well incorporated.
3. Now, spoon the mixture into lightly greased muffin cups. Lower the cups onto the rack in the Instant Pot.
4. Secure the lid. Choose "Manual" mode and High pressure; cook for 10 minutes. Once cooking is complete, use a natural pressure release; carefully remove the lid. Bon appétit!

Asian Saucy Duck Breast

Serves: 4

Cooking Time:2 Hours 15 Minutes

Ingredients:

- 2 tablespoons peanut oil
- 1/2 cup dry red wine
- 1/4 teaspoon Sichuan peppercorn powder
- 1 tablespoon sake
- 1/2 teaspoon coarse sea salt
- 1/2 cup chicken broth
- 1 pound duck breast, boneless, skinless and cut into 4 pieces
- 1/2 teaspoon cayenne pepper
- 2 garlic cloves, minced

Directions:

1. Place all ingredients, except for the broth, in the ceramic dish; place the dish in your refrigerator and let it marinate for 1 to 2 hours.
2. Then, transfer the meat along with its marinade to the Instant Pot. Pour in the chicken broth.
3. Secure the lid. Choose "Manual" mode and High pressure; cook for 10 minutes. Once cooking is complete, use a quick pressure release; carefully remove the lid.
4. Serve warm and enjoy!

BEANS & GRAINS RECIPES

Cauliflower Risotto

Serves: 8
Cooking Time: 33 Minutes

Ingredients:
- 2 small heads of cauliflower, cut in chunks
- 6 tablespoons olive oil, divided
- Salt and freshly ground black pepper, to taste
- 1 cup freshly grated Parmesan cheese, divided
- 2 tablespoons olive oil
- 2 large onions, diced
- 4 garlic cloves, minced
- 2 cups pearl barley
- 6 cups vegetable or chicken broth
- 4 sprigs thyme2 tablespoons butter
- 4 tablespoons chopped fresh parsley to garnish optional

Directions:
1. Add the oil, garlic and onion to the Instant Pot. "Sauté" for 3 minutes.
2. Stir in cauliflower chunks and "Sauté" for 5 minutes.
3. Add all the remaining ingredients to the cooker, except the cheese and butter.
4. Cover and secure the lid. Turn its pressure release handle to the sealing position.
5. Cook on the "Manual" function with high pressure for 25 minutes.
6. After the beep, do a Natural release and remove the lid.
7. Stir in butter and cheese.
8. Serve warm.

Tarragon Green Peas

Serves: 4
Cooking Time:20 Minutes

Ingredients:

- 1 (10-oz) bag frozen green peas
- 2 garlic cloves, minced
- 1/2 teaspoon dried tarragon
- 1/2 teaspoon dried dill
- 1 cups cream of mushroom soup
- 1 cup tomato sauce
- 2 teaspoons avocado oil
- 1 shallot, chopped
- 2 cup water
- Kosher salt and freshly ground black pepper, to taste

Directions:

1. Press the "Sauté" button and heat the oil. Once hot, cook the shallot until tender and translucent; add the garlic to the inner pot and continue sautéing an additional 30 seconds.
2. Now, stir in the remaining ingredients.
3. Secure the lid. Choose the "Manual" mode and cook for 12 minutes at High pressure. Once cooking is complete, use a quick pressure release; carefully remove the lid.
4. Ladle into soup bowls. Bon appétit!

Pinto Beans With Rice And Herbs

Serves: 6

Cooking Time:30 Minutes

Ingredients:

- 1 cup dry pinto beans
- 1 cup dry brown rice
- 2 tablespoons fresh chives, roughly chopped
- 3 cups water
- 1 tablespoon fresh rosemary, chopped
- 1 tablespoon fresh mint, chopped
- 3 bouillon cubes
- 1 tablespoon fresh parsley, chopped
- 1 ancho chili pepper, chopped
- 2 tomatoes, puréed
- 2 tablespoons olive oil

Directions:

1. Add all ingredients, except for the chives, to your Instant Pot.
2. Secure the lid. Choose the "Bean/Chili" mode and High pressure; cook for 25 minutes. Once cooking is complete, use a natural pressure release; carefully remove the lid.
3. Garnish with the chopped chives and enjoy!

Greek Gigante Beans

Serves: 5
Cooking Time: 30 Minutes

Ingredients:

- 3 cups dried Gigantes beans
- 8 cups water
- 1 ½ teaspoon salt
- ¼ cup extra virgin olive oil
- 1 clove of garlic, minced
- 1 onion, chopped
- 1 stalk of celery, chopped
- 1 can crushed tomatoes
- 1 teaspoon dried oregano
- ½ cup water
- ½ cup feta cheese, crumbled

Directions:

1. Place the beans, water, and salt in the Instant Pot.
2. Close the lid and press the Manual button. Adjust the cooking time to 15 minutes.
3. Once done, drain the beans then set aside. Clean the inner pot and place it back into the Instant Pot.
4. Press the Sauté button and heat the oil. Stir in the garlic, onions, and celery. Stir until fragrant.
5. Add in the beans, crushed tomatoes, and oregano. Pour in the water.
6. Close the lid and press the Manual button. Cook for another 15 minutes.
7. Do natural pressure release.
8. Top with feta cheese.

Chickpea & Jalapeño Chicken Stew

Serves: 6

Cooking Time: 40 Minutes

Ingredients:

- 1 pound boneless, skinless chicken legs
- 2 tbsp ground cumin
- ½ tbsp cayenne pepper
- 2 tbsp olive oil
- 1 onion, minced
- 2 jalapeño peppers, deseeded and minced
- 3 garlic cloves, crushed
- 2 tbsp freshly grated ginger
- ¼ cup chicken stock
- 1 (24 oz) can crushed tomatoes
- 2 (14 oz) cans chickpeas, drained and rinsed
- Salt to taste
- ½ cup coconut milk
- ¼ cup fresh parsley, chopped
- 2 cups hot cooked basmati rice

Directions:

1. Season the chicken with 1 tbsp salt, cayenne pepper, and cumin. Set on Sauté and warm the oil. Add in jalapeño peppers, and onion, and cook for 5 minutes until soft. Mix in ginger and garlic, and cook for 3 minutes until tender.
2. Add ¼ cup chicken stock into the cooker to ensure the pan is deglazed, from the pan's bottom scrape any browned bits of food.
3. Mix the onion mixture with, chickpeas, tomatoes, and salt. Stir in seasoned chicken to coat in sauce. Seal the lid and cook on High Pressure for 20 minutes. Release the pressure quickly.
4. Remove the chicken and slice into chunks. Into the remaining sauce, mix in coconut milk; simmer for 5 minutes on Keep Warm. Split rice into 4 bowls. Top with chicken, then sauce and add parsley for garnish.

Creamy Fettuccine With Ground Beef

Serves: 6

Cooking Time: 20 Minutes

Ingredients:

- 10 oz ground beef
- 1 lb fettuccine pasta
- 1 cup cheddar cheese, shredded
- 1 cup fresh spinach, torn
- 1 medium onion, chopped
- 2 cups tomatoes, diced
- 1 tbsp butter
- Salt and black pepper to taste

Directions:

1. Melt butter on Sauté. Stir-fry the beef and onion for 5 minutes. Add the pasta. Pour water enough to cover and season with salt and pepper. Cook on High Pressure for 5 minutes. Do a quick release. Press Sauté and stir in the tomatoes and spinach. Cook for 5 minutes. Top with shredded cheddar and serve.

Chili Black Bean & Rice Bowl

Serves: 4

Cooking Time: 50 Minutes

Ingredients:

- 2 tsp olive oil
- 1 clove garlic, minced
- 1 onion, diced
- ½ cup brown rice
- ½ cup black beans, soaked
- 2 cups water
- ½ tsp salt
- 1 avocado, sliced
- 2 tbsp chili-garlic sauce

Directions:

1. Warm olive oil in your Instant Pot on Sauté. Place in garlic and onion and cook for 2 minutes. Stir in rice and black beans. Add in water and salt and seal the lid. Select Manual and cook for 25 minutes on High pressure.
2. When over, allow a natural release for 10 minutes and unlock the lid. Drizzle with chili-garlic sauce and top with avocado. Serve immediately.

FISH & SEAFOOD RECIPES

Cheddar Haddock

Serves: 2
Cooking Time: 20 Minutes

Ingredients:
- 1 lb fresh or frozen haddock fillets
- 1 tbsp butter
- 1 tbsp flour
- ¼ tsp salt
- Ground black pepper to taste
- ½ cup milk
- 1 cup parmesan cheese, grated
- 1 cup water

Directions:
1. To preheat the Instant Pot, select SAUTÉ. Add the butter and melt it.
2. Add the flour, salt and pepper, stir well. Sauté for 1 minute.
3. Gradually pour the milk, cook for 3-5 minutes, stirring occasionally, until the sauce is smooth and thick.
4. Add the cheese to the pot and stir.
5. Press the CANCEL key to stop the SAUTÉ function.
6. In a pan, combine the fish fillets with sauce. Cover tightly with foil.
7. Clean the inner pot with water.
8. Pour a cup of water into the pot and set a steam rack in it.
9. Place the pan on the steam rack.
10. Select MANUAL and cook at HIGH pressure for 5 minutes.
11. Once pressure cooking is complete, use a Quick Release. Unlock and carefully open the lid.
12. Serve.

Bell Pepper & Cod With Millet

Serves: 2-4

Cooking Time:　20 Minutes

Ingredients:

- 1 tbsp olive oil
- 1 cup millet
- 1 yellow bell pepper, diced
- 1 red bell pepper, diced
- 2 cups chicken broth
- 1 cup breadcrumbs
- 4 tbsp melted butter
- ¼ cup minced fresh cilantro
- 1 tsp salt
- 4 cod fillets

Directions:

1. Combine oil, millet, yellow and red bell peppers in the pot, and cook for 1 minute on Sauté. Mix in the chicken broth. Place a trivet atop. In a bowl, mix crumbs, butter, cilantro, lemon zest, juice, and salt.
2. Spoon the breadcrumb mixture evenly on the cod fillet. Lay the fish on the trivet. Seal the lid and cook on High for 6 minutes. Do a quick release and serve immediately.

Vegetable Salmon Skewers

Serves: 4

Cooking Time:15 Minutes

Ingredients:

- 1 pound salmon, skinned, deboned and cut into bite-sized chunks
- 1 red onion, cut into wedges
- 2 bell peppers, cut into strips
- 1 teaspoon red pepper flakes
- 8 sticks fresh rosemary, lower leaves removed
- 2 tablespoons toasted sesame oil
- Sea salt and ground black pepper, to taste
- 1/2 pound yellow squash zucchini, cubed

Directions:

1. Prepare your Instant Pot by adding 1½ cups of water and metal rack to its bottom.
2. Thread the vegetables and fish alternately onto rosemary sticks.
3. Drizzle with the sesame oil; sprinkle with salt, black pepper, and red pepper flakes. Cover with a piece of foil.
4. Secure the lid. Choose "Manual" mode and Low pressure; cook for 6 minutes. Once cooking is complete, use a quick pressure release; carefully remove the lid. Serve immediately.

Salmon Curry

Serves: 8
Cooking Time: 12 Minutes

Ingredients:

- 3 lbs. salmon fillets cut into pieces2 tablespoons olive oil
- 2 Serrano peppers, chopped
- 1 teaspoon ground turmeric
- 4 tablespoons curry powder
- 4 teaspoons ground cumin
- 4 curry leaves
- 4 teaspoons ground coriander
- 2 small yellow onions, chopped
- 2 teaspoons red chili powder4 garlic cloves, minced
- 4 cups unsweetened coconut milk
- 2 ½ cups tomatoes, chopped
- 2 tablespoons fresh lemon juice
- Fresh cilantro leaves to garnish

Directions:

1. Put the oil and curry leaves to the insert of the Instant Pot. Select the "Sauté" function to cook for 30 secs.
2. Add the garlic and onions to the pot, cook for 5 minutes.
3. Stir in all the spices and cook for another 1 minute.
4. Put the fish, Serrano pepper, coconut milk, and tomatoes while cooking.
5. Cover and lock the lid. Seal the pressure release valve.
6. Select the "Manual" function at low pressure for 5 minutes.
7. After the beep, do a "Natural" release to release all the steam.
8. Remove the lid and squeeze in lemon juice.
9. Garnish with fresh cilantro leaves and serve.

Easy Mahi Mahi With Enchilada Sauce

Serves: 2

Cooking Time: 8 Minutes

Ingredients:

- 2 fresh Mahi Mahi fillets
- ¼ cup commercial enchilada sauce
- Salt and pepper, to taste
- 2 tbsps. butter

Directions:

1. Add all the ingredients, except for the butter, to the Instant Pot.
2. Lock the lid. Select the Manual mode and cook for 8 minutes at Low Pressure.
3. Once cooking is complete, do a quick pressure release. Carefully open the lid.
4. Stir in the butter and serve on plates.

Clam & Prawn Paella

Serves: 2-4

Cooking Time:　30 Minutes

Ingredients:

- 2 tbsp olive oil
- 1 onion, chopped
- 4 garlic cloves, minced
- ½ cup dry white wine
- 2 cups bomba (Spanish) rice
- 4 cups chicken stock
- 1 ½ tsp sweet paprika
- 1 tsp turmeric powder
- ½ tsp ground black pepper
- ½ tsp salt
- 1 pound small clams, scrubbed
- 1 lb fresh prawns, peeled and deveined
- 1 red bell pepper, diced
- 1 lemon, cut in wedges

Directions:

1. Stir-fry onion and garlic in a tbsp of oil on Sauté mode for 3 minutes. Pour in wine to deglaze, scraping the bottom of the pot of any brown. Cook for 2 minutes, until the wine is reduced by half.
2. Add in rice and water. Season with the paprika, turmeric, salt, and pepper. Seal the lid and cook on High Pressure for 10 minutes. Do a quick release. Remove to a plate and wipe the pot clean.
3. Heat the remaining oil on Sauté. Cook clams and prawns for 6 minutes, until the clams have opened and the shrimp are pink. Discard unopened clams. Arrange seafood and lemon wedges over paella, to serve.

Favorite Seafood Chowder

Serves: 4

Cooking Time: 45 Minutes

Ingredients:

- 6 oz mackerel fillets
- ½ cup wheat groats, soaked
- ½ cup kidney beans, soaked
- ¼ cup sweet corn
- 1 lb tomatoes, peeled, roughly chopped
- 4 cups fish stock
- 4 tbsp olive oil
- 1 tsp sea salt
- 1 tsp fresh rosemary, finely chopped
- 2 garlic cloves, crushed

Directions:

1. Heat olive oil on Sauté, and stir-fry tomatoes and garlic for 5 minutes. Add rosemary, stock, salt, corn, kidney beans, and wheat groats. Seal the lid and cook on High Pressure for 25 minutes.
2. Do a quick release and add mackerel fillets. Seal the lid and cook on Steam for 8 minutes on High. Do a quick release, open the lid and serve immediately drizzled with freshly squeezed lemon juice.

SOUPS, STEWS & CHILIS RECIPES

Bacon And Veggie Soup

Serves: 3
Cooking Time: 20 Minutes

Ingredients:
- ½ tablespoon olive oil
- ½ small yellow onion, chopped
- 1 garlic clove, minced
- ½ head cauliflower, chopped roughly
- ½ green bell pepper, seeded and choppedSalt, and freshly ground black pepper to taste
- 2 cups homemade chicken broth
- 1 cup Cheddar cheese, shredded
- ½ cup half-and-half cream*
- 3 cooked turkey bacon slices, chopped
- 2 dashes hot pepper sauce

Directions:
1. Add the oil with onion and garlic in the instant pot and "Sauté" for 3 minutes
2. Stir in the broth, salt, black pepper, cauliflower and bell pepper then secure the lid.
3. Select the 'soup'" function and cook for 15 minutes.
4. After the beep, 'quick release' the steam then remove the lid.
5. Stir in the remaining ingredients and cook on the 'sauté' function for 5 minutes.
6. Serve hot.

Bacon And Potato Soup

Serves: 6
Cooking Time: 20 Minutes

Ingredients:

- 1 tbsp. olive oil
- 2 cups chicken stock
- ½ cup sour cream
- ½ cup chopped onion
- 1½ lbs. potatoes, chopped
- 4 halved bacon slices

Directions:

1. Set the Instant Pot to Sauté and heat the olive oil.
2. Add the bacon and cook for about 8 minutes until crispy.
3. Drain the bacon in paper towels and then chop. Set aside on a plate.
4. Add the chopped onion and sauté for 2 minutes or until translucent.
5. Add the potatoes and stock. Stir well.
6. Lock the lid. Select the Manual mode, then set the timer for 10 minutes at High Pressure.
7. Once the timer goes off, do a quick pressure release. Carefully open the lid.
8. Transfer the soup to a blender and purée until smooth.
9. Stir in the sour cream. Top with the cooked bacon and serve.

Homemade Spinach Dip

Serves: 2

Cooking Time: 10 Minutes

Ingredients:

- 1 cup cream cheese
- ½ cup baby spinach, rinsed, torn into pieces
- ½ cup mozzarella cheese
- ½ tsp Italian seasoning mix
- ½ tsp black pepper, ground
- ¼ cup scallions
- ½ cup vegetable broth

Directions:

1. Place all ingredients in a mixing bowl. Stir well and transfer to your instant pot. Seal the lid and cook on High Pressure for 5 minutes. Release the steam naturally, for 10 minutes. Serve with celery sticks, or chips.

Chicken & Potato Soup

Serves: 4
Cooking Time: 30 Minutes

Ingredients:

- 2 tbsp olive oil
- ½ pound chicken thighs
- 2 potatoes, cut into chunks
- 1 carrot, cut into chunks
- 1 yellow onion, diced
- 2 garlic cloves, minced
- 1 celery rib, chopped
- 4 cups chicken bone broth
- Salt and black pepper to taste
- 2 tbsp fresh parsley, chopped

Directions:

1. Heat oil in your Instant Pot on Sauté and cook onion, carrot, celery, and garlic for 3 minutes. Add in chicken and Sauté for 4-5 minutes. Pour in broth and potatoes and seal the lid. Select Manual and cook for 15 minutes on High.Once ready, allow a natural release for 10 minutes, then perform a quick pressure release and unlock the lid. Adjust the seasoning and top with parsley. Serve immediately.

Chicken Soup

Serves: 2
Cooking Time: 10 Minutes

Ingredients:

- 1 cup heavy whipping cream
- ¼ cup onions
- 1 garlic cloves, minced
- 2 packets skinned and deboned chicken breasts
- 1 tbsp. ghee
- 3 cups water

Directions:

1. Combine all the ingredients, except for the heavy whipping cream, in the Instant Pot.
2. Lock the lid. Select the Manual mode, then set the timer for 6 minutes at High Pressure.
3. Once the timer goes off, do a natural pressure release for 5 minutes, then release any remaining pressure. Carefully open the lid.
4. Remove the chicken from the pot and transfer to a platter to shred it into pieces using forks.
5. Return it to the Instant Pot and add the heavy whipping cream to the soup. Stir to blend ingredients.
6. Serve warm.

Chicken Spinach Corn Soup

Serves: 5

Cooking Time: 10 Minutes

Ingredients:

- 1 tablespoon olive oil
- 2 medium chicken breasts, thinly sliced
- 3 scallions, chopped
- 1 large white potato, peeled and diced
- 1 tablespoon green onion, chopped1 tablespoon ginger, grated3 cups frozen corn kernels
- 4 cups chicken broth
- 1 tablespoon fish sauce
- 2 tablespoons light soy sauce
- 2 large cloves of garlic, diced
- ⅓ teaspoon white pepper1 teaspoon salt
- 1 tablespoon arrowroot powder3-4 handfuls of baby spinach leaves
- 2 eggs

Directions:

1. Add the oil, green onions, chicken, potato, scallions and ginger, into the instant pot and stir fry on the 'sauté' function for 5 minutes.
2. Place the corn kernels and 1 cup chicken broth into a blender. Blend well to form a smooth puree.
3. Now put the remaining ingredients and corn mixture into the cooker and secure the lid.
4. Cook for 5 minutes at high pressure on 'manual' function.
5. After the beep, 'natural release' the steam and remove the lid.
6. Switch the cooker to the 'sauté' mode.
7. Crack the eggs into a small bowl and whisk them well. Pour the egg mix into the soup, stirring constantly.
8. Dissolve the arrowroot powder in water and stir it into the soup.
9. Cook for 1 minute then serve hot.

Chicken Moringa Soup

Serves: 6-8
Cooking Time: 45 Minutes

Ingredients:
- 1½ lbs chicken breasts
- 5 cups water
- 1 onion, chopped
- 2 cloves garlic, minced
- 1 cup tomatoes, chopped
- 1 thumb-size ginger
- 2 cups moringa leaves or kale leaves
- Salt and ground black pepper to taste

Directions:
1. Combine all of the ingredients, except moringa leaves, in the Instant Pot and stir to mix.
2. Close and lock the lid. Press the POULTRY button and set the cooking time for 15 minutes.
3. When the timer beeps, let the pressure Release Naturally for 15 minutes, then release any remaining steam manually. Open the lid.
4. Add the moringa leaves and stir. Select SAUTÉ and simmer for 3 minutes.
5. Taste for seasoning and add more salt if needed. Serve.

TURKEY RECIPES

Herb Turkey Breast

Serves: 6
Cooking Time: 50 Minutes

Ingredients:
- 3 lbs turkey breast
- 2 cups chicken broth
- 2 sprigs fresh rosemary
- 1 sprig fresh thyme
- 1 tsp salt
- ½ tsp ground black pepper
- 1 tsp dried oregano
- 1 tsp dried basil
- 1 red onion, quartered
- 3 stalks celery, roughly chopped

Directions:
1. Prepare the Instant Pot by adding the broth to the pot and placing the steam rack in it.
2. Add the rosemary and thyme to the pot
3. Season the turkey with salt, pepper, dried oregano, and dried basil.
4. Place the meat on the steam rack, breast side up. Add the onion and celery.
5. Close and lock the lid. Select MANUAL and cook at HIGH pressure for 35 minutes.
6. When the timer beeps, select CANCEL and let Naturally Release for 10 minutes. Open the lid.
7. Transfer the turkey to a serving bowl and slice it. Serve with the gravy.

Herbed Turkey Meatloaf

Serves: 5
Cooking Time: 40 Minutes

Ingredients:

- 1 tablespoon olive oil
- 1 shallot, minced
- 1 ½ pounds ground turkey
- 1/2 cup Romano cheese, grated
- 1/3 cup fine breadcrumbs
- 1 egg, whisked
- Sea salt and ground black pepper, to taste
- 1 tablespoon garlic and herb seasoning blend
- 1/2 cup ketchup
- 1 teaspoon molasses
- 1 teaspoon Dijon mustard
- 1 tablespoon soy sauce

Directions:

1. Press the "Sauté" button to preheat your Instant Pot. Heat the oil and sauté the shallot until tender and aromatic.
2. Add the ground turkey, cheese, breadcrumbs, egg, salt, pepper, and herb seasoning blend. Shape the mixture into a meatloaf and wrap it into a piece of foil.
3. Mix the ketchup, molasses, mustard and soy sauce in a small bowl. Pour the mixture on top of the meatloaf, spreading it into an even layer.
4. Place a steamer rack and 1/2 cup of water inside the inner pot. Lower your meatloaf onto the steamer rack.
5. Secure the lid. Choose the "Poultry" mode and cook for 30 minutes at High pressure. Once cooking is complete, use a quick pressure release; carefully remove the lid.
6. Let your meatloaf stand for 10 minutes before cutting and serving. Bon appétit!

Turkey Breasts With Bacon And Gravy

Serves: 4

Cooking Time: 35 Minutes

Ingredients:

- 1 tablespoon butter, melted
- 1 ½ pounds turkey breasts, boneless and skinless
- 4 rashers smoked bacon
- 2 garlic cloves, minced
- 1 teaspoon onion powder
- Salt, to taste
- 1/2 teaspoon mixed peppercorns, crushed
- 2 sweet peppers, sliced
- 1 cup cherry wine
- 1 cup chicken stock
- 1 tablespoon arrowroot powder

Directions:

1. Press the "Sauté" button to preheat your Instant Pot. Melt the butter and cook the turkey breasts for 4 to 6 minutes until golden brown on both sides.
2. Top with the bacon; add the garlic, onion powder, salt, and crushed peppercorns. Add the sweet peppers.
3. Pour in the wine and chicken stock and secure the lid.
4. Choose the "Manual" mode and cook for 25 minutes at High pressure. Once cooking is complete, use a quick pressure release; carefully remove the lid.
5. Press the "Sauté" button again and thicken the pan juices with the arrowroot powder. Spoon the gravy over the turkey breasts and serve immediately. Bon appétit!

Turkey Verde And Rice

Serves: 6-8

Cooking Time: 35 Minutes

Ingredients:

- 1½ lbs turkey tenderloins
- 1 tbsp olive oil
- 1 small onion, sliced
- ½ cup brown rice, long grain
- ½ cup salsa verde
- 1 cup chicken broth
- ½ tsp salt

Directions:

1. Select the SAUTÉ setting on the Instant Pot and heat the oil.
2. Add the onion. Stir and sauté for 3-4 minutes until the onion is translucent.
3. Add the rice, salsa verde, broth, and salt. Stir well.
4. Press the CANCEL button to reset the cooking program.
5. Close and lock the lid. Select the MANUAL setting and set the cooking time for 18 minutes at HIGH pressure.
6. Once cooking is complete, let the pressure Release Naturally for 10 minutes. Release any remaining steam manually. Uncover the pot.
7. Transfer the turkey to a plate and slice the meat. Serve with rice.

Simple Turkey Breast Roast

Serves: 4

Cooking Time: 60 Minutes

Ingredients:
- 1 (3 lbs) turkey breast roast, boneless
- 2 tbsp + 2 tbsp garlic infused oil
- 2 tsp salt
- 1½ cups chicken broth

Directions:
1. Rub all sides of the turkey with 2 tablespoons of oil and season with salt.
2. Preheat the Instant Pot by selecting SAUTÉ. Add the remaining oil.
3. Put the meat in the pot and brown on both sides. Press the CANCEL button to stop SAUTE function.
4. Transfer the turkey breast roast to a bowl.
5. Add the broth to the pot and deglaze the pot by scraping the bottom to remove all of the brown bits.
6. Insert the steam rack. Place the turkey meat on top.
7. Close and lock the lid. Select the MANUAL setting and set the cooking time for 30 minutes at HIGH pressure.
8. Once cooking is complete, select CANCEL and use a Natural Release for 10 minutes. Release any remaining steam manually. Open the lid.
9. Serve.

Turkey With Bean Chili

Serves: 4
Cooking Time: 50 Minutes

Ingredients:

- 1 lb ground turkey
- 1 tbsp olive oil
- 2 cups onion, diced
- ½ cup Anaheim pepper, diced
- ½ cup red bell pepper, diced
- 1 cup cannellini beans, soaked for 8 hours
- 2½ cups chicken stock
- 1 tsp oregano
- 2 tbsp chili powder
- 1 tbsp salt
- ½ tsp black pepper
- 3 tbsp cilantro leaves, chopped

Directions:

1. Preheat the Instant Pot by selecting SAUTÉ. Add the oil.
2. Add the onion, Anaheim pepper, and bell pepper and sauté until the vegetables are translucent.
3. Add the ground turkey, beans, chicken stock, oregano, chili powder, salt, and black pepper. Stir well. Close and lock the lid.
4. Press the CANCEL button to reset the cooking program, then select the BEAN/CHILI setting and set the cooking time for 30 minutes.
5. When the timer beeps, let the pressure Release Naturally for 10 minutes, then release any remaining steam manually. Open the pot.
6. Top with cilantro leaves and serve.

Turkey And Barley Tabbouleh

Serves: 4

Cooking Time: 20 Minutes

Ingredients:

- 1 pound turkey breast fillet, slice into bite-sized pieces
- 1 cup pearl barley
- 1 bay leaf
- 2 carrots, trimmed and thinly sliced
- 2 ½ cups vegetable broth
- 1 bunch spring onions, thinly sliced
- 1 medium cucumber, sliced
- 2 medium vine-ripened tomatoes, sliced
- 1 garlic clove, crushed
- 1 tablespoon harissa paste
- 2 limes, freshly squeezed
- 4 tablespoons extra-virgin olive oil
- 1/4 teaspoon freshly ground black pepper
- Pink salt, to taste

Directions:

1. Add the turkey breast fillets, barley, bay leaf, carrots, and vegetable broth to the inner pot.
2. Secure the lid. Choose the "Manual" mode and cook for 9 minutes at High pressure. Once cooking is complete, use a quick pressure release; carefully remove the lid.
3. Drain, chill and transfer to a serving bowl. Add the spring onions, cucumber, tomatoes, and garlic to the bowl.
4. In a small mixing dish, thoroughly combine the remaining ingredients. Drizzle this dressing over your salad and serve immediately. Bon appétit!

OTHER INSTANT POT RECIPES

Bourbon Pudding Cake With Dates

Serves: 4

Cooking Time: 50 Minutes

Ingredients:

- ½ tsp baking soda
- ½ tsp cinnamon powder
- ¼ tsp cloves powder
- ¼ tsp allspice
- ¼ tsp salt
- ¾ cup plain flour
- 1 tsp baking powder
- 6 tbsp hot water
- 2 tbsp bourbon
- 3 tbsp unsalted butter, melted
- 2 tbsp whole milk
- 1 egg, lightly beaten
- ½ cup chopped dates
- ½ cup salted caramel sauce for topping

Directions:

1. In a medium bowl, combine baking soda, cinnamon, cloves, allspice, salt, flour, and baking powder. In another bowl, mix hot water, bourbon, butter, and milk. Pour into dry ingredients and mix until well-mixed. Whisk in egg and then fold in the dates.

2. Lightly grease 4 medium ramekins with cooking spray, divide mixture among them, and cover with foil. Pour 1 cup of water in inner pot, fit in a trivet with slings, and place ramekins on top. Seal the lid, select Manual/Pressure Cook mode on High, and set cooking time to 25 minutes.

3. After cooking, perform a natural pressure release for 10 minutes, then a quick pressure release to let out the steam. Unlock the lid and carefully remove ramekins, invert onto dessert plates, and drizzle caramel sauce on top. Serve.

Pork With Jalapeño Sauce & Velveeta Cheese

Serves: 4
Cooking Time: 30 Minutes

Ingredients:
- 2 tbsp olive oil
- 1 lb ground pork
- Salt and black pepper to taste
- 1 cup milk
- 1 cup white Velveeta cheese
- 1 (16 oz) jar salsa verde
- 16 oz sour cream
- 2 jalapeño peppers, sliced

Directions:
1. Set your Instant Pot to Sauté and heat olive oil. Cook pork until brown, 5 minutes. Season with a little salt and black pepper. Add in milk and seal the lid. Select Manual/Pressure Cook, and set time to 15 minutes. When ready, do a quick pressure release.
2. Press Sauté, mix in Velveeta cheese, salsa verde, sour cream, and jalapeño peppers. Cook with frequent stirring until cheese melts. Dish into serving bowls and serve warm.

Instant Pot Egg Custard

Serves: 6
Cooking Time: 10 Minutes

Ingredients:

- 4 cups of milk
- 6 large eggs, beaten
- ¾ cup white sugar
- 1 teaspoon vanilla extract
- A pinch of salt
- ¼ teaspoon ground cinnamon

Directions:

1. Place a trivet or steamer basket inside the Instant Pot and pour water over.
2. In a mixing bowl, combine all ingredients. Whisk until well-combined.
3. Place the egg mixture into a baking dish that will fit inside the Instant Pot. Cover with aluminum foil.
4. Place the baking dish with the egg mixture on the steamer basket.
5. Close the lid.6. Press the Manual button and adjust the cooking time to 10 minutes.
6. Do natural pressure release.

Hot Paprika And Pork Omelet

Serves: 2
Cooking Time: 25 Minutes

Ingredients:

- 1 tablespoon canola oil
- 1/2 pound ground pork
- 1 yellow onion, thinly sliced
- 1 red chili pepper, minced
- 4 eggs, whisked
- 1/2 teaspoon garlic powder
- 1/3 teaspoon cumin powder
- 1 teaspoon oyster sauce
- Kosher salt and ground black pepper, to taste
- 1/2 teaspoon paprika

Directions:

1. Press the "Sauté" button and heat the oil until sizzling; once hot, cook the ground pork until no longer pink, crumbling with a spatula.
2. Add the onion and pepper; cook an additional 2 minutes. Whisk the eggs with the remaining ingredients. Pour the egg mixture over the meat mixture in the inner pot.
3. Secure the lid. Choose the "Manual" mode and cook for 8 minutes at High pressure. Once cooking is complete, use a natural pressure release for 10 minutes; carefully remove the lid. Bon appétit!

Sage Pork Chops With Apple Sauce

Serves: 4

Cooking Time: 55 Minutes

Ingredients:

- 2 tbsp olive oil
- 4 bone-in pork chops
- Salt and black pepper to taste
- 2 garlic cloves, minced
- 2 tbsp chopped sage
- 1 lb apples, peeled and sliced
- 3 tbsp butter
- 4 tbsp honey
- ½ cup apple cider vinegar
- ½ cup chicken broth
- ½ cup heavy cream
- 2 tbsp chopped parsley

Directions:

1. Set your Instant Pot to Sauté. Heat olive oil, season pork with salt and pepper, and sear in oil until golden brown on the outside, 6 minutes. Set aside. Add garlic and sage to oil and stir-fry until fragrant, 30 seconds. Pour in apples, butter, and honey; cook until apples caramelize, 5 minutes. Top with apple cider vinegar, broth, and pork.
2. Seal the lid, select Manual/Pressure Cook mode on High, and set cooking time to 20 minutes. After cooking, perform a natural pressure release for 10 minutes. Unlock the lid and stir in heavy cream. Simmer in Sauté mode for 2 to 3 minutes. Spoon food into serving plates with a generous topping of sauce. Garnish with parsley and serve warm.

Italian Chicken Soup With Artichokes

Serves: 4
Cooking Time: 45 Minutes

Ingredients:

- 2 tbsp olive oil
- 1 yellow onion, chopped
- 2 celery stalks, chopped
- 2 large carrots, chopped
- 5 garlic cloves, minced
- 2 chicken breasts, cut into ½-inch cubes
- 4 cups chicken stock
- 2 tsp Italian seasoning
- 2 bay leaves
- Salt and black pepper to taste
- ½ tsp chili powder
- ½ lemon, juiced
- 3 cups chopped artichoke hearts
- ¼ cup vermicelli

Directions:

1. Set your Instant Pot to Sauté mode. Heat olive oil in inner pot, sauté onion, celery, carrots, and cook until softened, 3 minutes. Stir in garlic until softened, 3 minutes. Mix in chicken breasts, stock, Italian seasoning, bay leaves, salt, pepper, and chili powder. Seal the lid, select Manual/Pressure Cook on High, and set time to 10 minutes.
2. After cooking, perform a natural pressure release for 10 minutes, then a quick pressure release to let out remaining steam, and unlock the lid. Mix in lemon juice, artichoke, and vermicelli and cook further 5 minutes on Sauté. Dish soup and serve warm.

Thai Curry Rice With Chicken

Serves: 4

Cooking Time: 35 Minutes

Ingredients:

- 4 chicken thighs
- Salt and black pepper to taste
- 1 tbsp olive oil
- 2 medium carrots, julienned
- 1 red bell pepper, deseeded and thinly sliced
- 2 tbsp red curry paste
- 1 garlic clove, minced
- 1 tsp ginger paste
- 2 cups basmati rice
- 3 cups chicken broth
- 1 cup coconut milk
- 2 tbsp chopped cilantro to garnish
- 1 lime, cut into wedges to garnish

Directions:

1. Set your Instant Pot to Sauté and adjust to medium heat. Heat olive oil in inner pot, season chicken with salt and black pepper, and sear in oil until golden brown on both sides, 6 minutes. Place on a plate and set aside.
2. Add carrots and bell pepper to oil and cook until softened, 4 minutes. Stir in curry paste, garlic, and ginger; sauté for 1 minute. Add rice, broth, coconut milk and give ingredients a good stir. Arrange chicken on top. Seal the lid, select Manual/Pressure Cook mode on High, and set cooking time to 10 minutes.
3. After cooking, do a natural pressure release for 10 minutes, then quick pressure release to let out remaining steam. Unlock the lid, fluff rice, and adjust taste with salt and black pepper. Garnish with cilantro, lime wedges, and serve.

RECIPES INDEX

Salmon Curry 75

Sausage & Spinach Rigatoni 41

Simple Turkey Breast Roast 90

Smoked Salmon And Green Bean Pilau 42

Spicy Red Lentils With Yogurt 23

T

Tarragon Green Peas 66

Tasty Asparagus Soup 44

Tasty Beef Neck Bone Stock 52

Thai Curry Rice With Chicken 99

Turkey And Barley Tabbouleh 92

Turkey Breasts With Bacon And Gravy 88

Turkey Verde And Rice 89

Turkey With Bean Chili 91

Two-cheese Cauliflower Muffins 63

V

Vegetable Bowl With Tahini Sauce 29

Vegetable Salmon Skewers 74

CPSIA information can be obtained
at www.ICGtesting.com
Printed in the USA
LVHW051339291122
734184LV00005B/478